GREAT
SCIENTISTS

THEIR LIVES AND CONTRIBUTIONS

LEE KHENG CHOOI

PARTRIDGE

Library of Congress Control Number:		2020905799
ISBN:	Softcover	978-1-5437-5761-3
	eBook	978-1-5437-5762-0

Print information available on the last page.

To order additional copies of this book, contact
Toll Free 800 101 2657 (Singapore)
Toll Free 1 800 81 7340 (Malaysia)
orders.singapore@partridgepublishing.com

www.partridgepublishing.com/singapore

CONTENTS

Introduction vii

Chapter 1   Isaac Newton 1
Chapter 2   Michael Faraday 5
Chapter 3   Albert Einstein 9
Chapter 4   Paul Dirac 15
Chapter 5   Richard Feynman 19
Chapter 6   Albert A. Michelson 23
Chapter 7   Werner Heisenberg...................................27
Chapter 8   Ernest Rutherford....................................33

Conclusion 37

INTRODUCTION

Many of us think of scientists as men and women in white lab coats looking through a microscope. The truth is that the lab coat only made its first appearance in the 1800s; therefore, Isaac Newton, born in 1600, most likely did not don one.

You are probably familiar with things like refrigerators, electric motors, Li-on batteries, and radio receivers, but do you know the great scientists behind these inventions that we enjoy in our modern world?

In this book, we will explore some of the greatest scientists, giving you an insight into their lives and contributions to the world. Perhaps reading this book will inspire you in your self-discovery or simply give you a deeper appreciation for the scientists who have made our world a better place with their contributions.

"The saddest aspect of life right now is that science gathers knowledge faster than society gathers wisdom." -Isaac Asimov

CHAPTER 1

ISAAC NEWTON

"I can calculate the motion of heavenly bodies, but not the madness of people." -Isaac Newton

4 January 1643 - 31 March 1727

<u>Early life</u>

Sir Isaac Newton was born in Woolsthorpe, England. His father was a farmer also named Isaac Newtown, but he died three months before his birth, and his mother was Hannah Ayscough. Newton was said to be born premature and so small size that he could fit inside a mug. Newton's mother Hannah remarried when he was three-years-old, and she left Newton in the care of his maternal grandmother when she went to live with her new husband, Reverend Barnabas Smith. Newton was said to have misgivings for his stepfather and mother, as revealed in some of his writings. Being left behind at such a young age caused him to have insecurities throughout his life.

Education

From twelve to seventeen, Newton studied with a chemist and was introduced to chemistry at The King's School, Grantham. However, his mother, who was widowed a second time, pulled him out of school and tried to make him a farmer. It was a disaster as Newton hated farming; he found it boring. Fortunately, the schoolmaster persuaded Newton's mother to let him continue his education. Newton became a top student who excelled in constructing models of windmills and sundials (clocks).

In June 1661, Newton entered the Trinity College, Cambridge, as an undergraduate, working his way to pay for food and education until he received a scholarship in 1664 for his Master of Arts. Like most students of his generation, Newton was immersed in the works of Aristotle, and popular philosophers like Rene Descartes, and astronomers, Thomas Street, and Galileo. In 1665, Newton's studies were interrupted for two years by the Great Plague of London, and he returned home to work on his theories regarding light, color, and calculus. It was during this time that his family farm became the famous setting for the myth of the falling apple that transpired his theory on the law of gravity.

Career

After returning to his studies, Newton was elected as a fellow of the Trinity but managed to avoid being ordained a priest through special permission from King Charles II. In 1672, Newton's discoveries in optics and light were so impressive he was elected a fellow to the Royal Society. He began to publish his theory of colors for the academics, and his theorized white light was the composite for all colors of the spectrum. Around this time, Newton became the Lucasian Professor at Cambridge and chose optics as his specialty using the telescope to prove his theory on color and light.

Critics

Although Newton's work was held in high esteem, there were also many critics of his work. One of the worst critics was a fellow member and rival Robert Hooke whom Newton had many exchanges over the years, to the point that he threatened to resign from the Royal Society. In 1678, Newton had a nervous breakdown, which was worsened by the death of his mother. For the next six years, Newton remained in isolation and minimized intellectual exchanges. He focused on his study of gravitation, which later came to fruition and was published in Principia. This caused Hooke to accuse Newton of plagiarism, but in truth, Hooke only theorized the idea without ever proving it. In 1703, Newton became the president of the Royal Society.

Principia

After eighteen months of intense work, Newton published his groundbreaking book 'Principia' in 1687. This book was also credited for providing the basic theory of calculus, thus making it the most influential physics book. It specified Newton's famous three laws of motion:

1. A resting object will stay at rest unless an external force is applied to it.
2. Force is equal to mass times acceleration (F = ma).
3. To every action, there is an equal and opposite reaction.

Principia not only raised Newton's prominence worldwide but also gave the three basic laws that helped Newton solidify his theory of gravity, which explained motion in the universe, such as the moon revolving around Earth, and comets orbiting around the sun.

Sir Isaac Newton

After Newton's publication of Principia, he lost interest in academic life in Cambridge. In 1689, he was elected to represent Cambridge in Parliament, although he did not resign from his post at Cambridge. Newton was named the warden of the Royal Mint in 1696, whereby he elevated the pound sterling to a gold standard and weeded out counterfeiters by sending them to the gallows. In 1705, Newton was knighted by Queen Anne.

Later years

Newton became famous and wealthy in his later years, although he never married. In his old age, Newton was living near Winchester with his niece, Catherine Conduitt, and her husband. Newton, considered as one of the most influential scientists, passed away in his sleep at eighty-four and was buried in Westminster Abbey.

Discoveries

- Gravity
- Laws of motion
- Calculus
- Reflecting telescope

CHAPTER 2

MICHAEL FARADAY

"No matter what you look at, if you look at it closely enough, you are involved in the entire universe." -Michael Faraday

22 September 1791 to 25 August 1867

<u>Early life</u>

Michael Faraday was born in Newington, Surrey London. His father, James Faraday, was a blacksmith, and his mother was a countrywoman. Faraday had three siblings, and they often did not have enough to eat because their father's poor health did not allow him to work regularly. Sometimes, Faraday had to survive one week with only a loaf of bread.

<u>Education</u>

Faraday only received a basic education. He was mostly self-educated through reading, writing, and Sunday school. From young, he earned money by delivering newspapers, and at fourteen as an apprentice to a local bookseller-cum-bookbinder. Faraday had the opportunity to devour many books during his seven-year apprenticeship with the bookbinder as he read all the books he had bound together. During this time, he developed an interest in science, electricity, and did his own simple experiments.

Early career

At twenty, Faraday was gifted tickets by a customer to attend Sir Humphry Davy's chemistry lectures at the Royal Institution of Great Britain. Later, Faraday sent his bound 300-page handwritten lecture notes to Davy in the hope of employment. Then, in 1813, Davy decided to hire Faraday as his assistant when he had to replace his current assistant, who was sacked for misconduct. Faraday, twenty-one, was given a good salary and a room at the institution. He began learning chemistry as a laboratory assistant under the guidance of one of the greatest practitioners; this also marked his long association with the Royal Institution for the next fifty-four years.

Mid-career and marriage.

In 1816, Faraday gave his first lecture on properties of matter and published his first academic paper on calcium hydroxide. Faraday's apprenticeship with Davy ended in 1920, and by then, he had developed his theories that would later become discoveries. A few years later, at twenty-nine, Faraday as a renowned chemist, was promoted to superintendent of the house and laboratory of the Royal Institution. Faraday married Sarah Barnard in June 1821, and they lived in the rooms of the institution for the next forty-six years. They had no children; both their families were from the Sandemanian church, a branch of the Church of Scotland. Faraday was a devout Christian, who served as a deacon and later as an elder of his church. Over the next few years, Faraday rose through the ranks from director to Fullerian Professor of chemistry at the Royal Institution when he was forty-one. He declined the position of president twice.

Later years

Faraday was given an honorary Doctor of Civil Law degree from the University of Oxford in 1832. He was also offered a knighthood, which he turned down for religious reasons. Subsequently, he was also an elected member to the American Academy of Arts and Sciences, the Royal Swedish Academy of Sciences, the French Academy of Sciences, and the Royal Institute of the Netherlands.

In 1839, Faraday had a nervous breakdown but recovered and returned to work on electromagnetism. In the 1840s, Faraday's health began to decline, and in 1855, Faraday began to sink into senility. He eventually retired in 1858 and lived in Master Mason's House, later called Faraday House, free of charge as a reward from Prince Albert (Queen Victoria's husband) for his lifetime service to science.

Faraday passed away at seventy-six and was buried in Highgate cemetery. He has been called the 'father of electricity,' along with Thomas Edison and Nikola Tesla. In June 1991, the Bank of England issued a £20 note with his portrait to honor his part in the progress of science in England, making Faraday part of famous Brits like Isaac Newton, William Shakespeare, and Florence Nightingale who also had their portraits on banknotes. Today, one can visit the Faraday Museum at the Royal Institution, which displays several of his most groundbreaking discoveries, such as the original Faraday disc, which is an early version of his electrostatic generators, the mega-size magnet, and chemical specimens.

Discoveries

- 1821 - Electromagnetic rotation, which would later evolve into the electric motor we know today.
- 1823 - Discovery of gas liquefaction, which would later form the basis of modern refrigerators.
- 1825 - Discovery of benzene, which is an essential substance in chemistry, and used for making new materials.
- 1831 - Discovery of electromagnetic induction. Most modern houses are powered using Faraday's principle of converting kinetic energy into electrical energy.
- 1834 - Laws of electrolysis, which is the science that produces our Li-on batteries and metal hydride batteries for mobile phones.
- 1836 - Faraday cages, which have been used to create dead zones for mobile communications.
- 1845 - Faraday effect, which established light in an electromagnetic wave.
- 1845 - Diamagnetism is a property of all matter. When diamagnetism in materials is induced by strong magnets, it can produce levitation in a strong magnetic field.

CHAPTER 3
ALBERT EINSTEIN

---

14 March 1879 - 18 April 1955

<u>Early life</u>

Albert Einstein was born in Ulm, Württemberg, Germany. His father was Hermann Einstein, an engineer, and salesman who founded a Munich based company with his brother manufacturing electrical equipment. Einstein's mother was Pauline Koch, and he had one younger sister Maja. They were brought up in a secular Jewish household.

<u>Education</u>

Einstein attended a Catholic elementary school in Munich at five-years-old, and three years later, he was transferred to Luitpold Gymnasium for his primary and secondary school education. In 1894, Einstein's family moved to Italy and later to Pavia when his father's business failed. However, Einstein, then fifteen, remained in a boarding school in Munich to finish his education, even though he struggled with his school's rigid teaching style. He had speech challenges but had a passion for classical music and the violin, which would stay with him throughout his life.

At sixteen, Einstein ran away, back to his parent's house, to avoid being drafted into military duty. They were unhappy with him as they realized that he'd have no prospects as a dropout and draft dodger. In 1911, Einstein gained entry to the Swiss Federal Polytechnic School in Zurich because of his exceptional math and physics scores, even though he did not have the strict entry requirement of a diploma. However, he had to finish his high school first in Aarau, Switzerland, and there he met his first love, Marie Winteler, the daughter of the schoolmaster.

In 1896, Einstein renounced his German citizenship to avoid military duties and became a Swiss citizen. Around that time, he entered the Zurich Polytechnic, where he took a physics and math teaching diploma program for four years. At the same time, Marie left to accept a teaching job at Olsberg.

Career

After graduating, Einstein could not find work and took small jobs tutoring children. He eventually found work as a patent clerk in a Swiss patent office in 1902. He worked on his ideas in the theory of relativity whenever he had free time.

In 1905, also known as Einstein's miracle year, he published four papers on the topics of the Brownian motion and photoelectric effect, the theory of relativity, and E=MC2 in a well-known physics journal. These papers became the turning point for Einstein's career and launched him in the course of modern physics. Owing to an endorsement by Max Planck, the founder of quantum theory, Einstein's papers became widely noticed. Soon he was regularly invited to lecture at international conferences, and his fame rose quickly in the academic world with job offers at prestigious institutions. From 1913 to 1933, Einstein accepted the post of director at the Kaiser Wilhelm Institute for Physics. In 1921, Einstein was given the Nobel Prize for Physics for his photoelectric effect.

Personal life

Einstein met his wife, Mileva Marić, a Serbian at the Polytechnic. They married in January 1903 and had two sons. The older son Hans became a well known hydraulic engineer. In 1914, they moved to Berlin, but his wife returned to Zurich with their sons when she discovered his affair with his cousin, Elsa Löwenthal. The couple divorced five years later in February 1919. Einstein married Elsa, that same year. Einstein was known to have several affairs throughout his second marriage to Elsa. The couple emigrated to the U.S. in 1933. Six years later, Elsa passed away from heart and kidney failure.

In 1987 early correspondence between Einstein and Marić was published, revealing that they had a daughter named Lieserl, born in 1902 in Novi Sad. The whereabouts of Lieserl was unknown as Marić returned to Switzerland without her. It was suspected that Lieserl was either adopted, raised by Marić relatives, or died from scarlet fever.

In 2015, correspondences between Einstein and his first love, Marie Winteler, were published. In the 1910 letter, Einstein wrote to profess his strong feelings for Marie while his wife was carrying their second son Eduard. He wrote about his missed chance with Marie and his misplaced feelings for his wife.

Einstein's son Eduard was diagnosed with schizophrenia when he was twenty. He was eventually committed to an asylum when his mother, Marić, passed away.

Later years

In the U.S., Einstein took a post at the Institute for Advanced Study at Princeton in 1933, where he spent the rest of his career. In 1940, Einstein became a U.S. citizen. During World War II, he was working on navy based weapon systems and giving donations to the military through the auctioning of his manuscripts. In 1939, the U.S. initiated the Manhattan Project to develop the atomic bomb, but Einstein was not directly involved in its development because of his pacifist beliefs. After the bombing of Hiroshima, Einstein worked with the United Nations to advocate using nuclear weapons only as a deterrent to conflict.

After World War II, Einstein continued working on his theory of relativity, time travel, black holes, wormholes, and origins of the universe. He started withdrawing from the spotlight, preferring to work in Princeton with his colleagues.

Einstein passed away at seventy-six, in the University Medical Center at Princeton after suffering an abdominal aortic aneurysm. At the hospital, he refused surgery, opting to accept his fate and, "go when I want." His body was cremated, and his ashes were scattered at a confidential place. His brain, however, was preserved for study at the Princeton University Medical Center.

Discoveries

- 1905 - Theory of relativity, which in layman terms means the more massive an object, the more it warps the space around it. This theory gave us a more accurate prediction of planetary orbiting around the sun.
- 1905 - E=MC2, which means the energy in a system, e.g., a person or atom (E) is equal to its total mass (M), multiplied by the speed of light squared (C2 - 186,000 miles per second). This equation suggested tiny particles of matter could be converted into huge energy. It was this theory that gave birth to the infamous atomic bomb used during World War II at Hiroshima and Nagasaki.

CHAPTER 4

PAUL DIRAC

"In science one tries to tell people, in such a way as to be understood by everyone, something that no one ever knew before. But in poetry, it's the exact opposite." -Paul Dirac

8 August 1902 - 20 October 1984

<u>Early life</u>

Paul Adrien Maurice Dirac was born in Bristol, England. His father, Charles Adrien Ladislas Dirac, was a Swiss immigrant who was a French teacher. His mother, Florence Hannah Dirac, was a librarian at the Bristol Central Library. Dirac had two siblings. They remained Swiss nationals until they were naturalized in 1919.

<u>Education</u>

Dirac was educated at Bishop Road Primary School, followed by the Merchant Venturer's Technical College, where his father worked. Later, Dirac won a scholarship to study electrical engineering at the University of Bristol. After graduating with his degree in 1921, Dirac entered into Cambridge but did not have enough money to live and study there. He accepted the offer to study for a Bachelor of Arts at the University of Bristol. In 1923, Dirac graduated again, and this time he received enough scholarship to study at Cambridge. At Cambridge, he pursued quantum physics and the theory of general relativity. Dirac received a research fellowship from 1925 to 1928. In June 1926, he received his Ph.D. with his first thesis on quantum mechanics.

Career

After receiving his Ph.D., Dirac became a fellow at St. John College in 1927. In 1932, he became the Lucasian professor of Mathematics at Cambridge for the next thirty-seven years. Dirac's work focused mainly on mathematical and the theory of quantum mechanics, as introduced by Heisenberg in 1925. He was an elected fellow of the Royal Society in 1930, receiving the society's royal medal, and the Copley medal. During this time, he traveled and studied at an extensive number of international universities. In 1933, he and Erwin Schrödinger shared the Nobel Prize for physics for their discovery of new productive forms of atomic theory. During World War II, Dirac worked on nuclear weapons and uranium separators.

Personal life

Dirac married Margit Wigner, the sister of physicist and mathematician, Eugene Wigner, in 1937 and adopted her two children, Gabriel and Judith. The couple had two children together named Mary and Florence. They met during a dinner at a restaurant while he was on a sabbatical at Princeton University.

It was said that Dirac could maintain his work productivity because Margit took care of everything. The couple later moved to Florida because Margit did not like Cambridge. As a person, Dirac was described by his colleagues as precise, introverted, and modest. Albert Einstein once described Dirac as being a balance of madness and genius.

Years after his death, it was speculated that Dirac had undiagnosed Asperger's syndrome or autism, which might have explained his extreme introversion, lack of empathy, and rigid behavior. It was said that Dirac only cried once, and that was when he learned that his friend, Einstein, had died. Known for his long silences, his colleagues at Cambridge jokingly coined a new unit called 'Dirac' and defined it as one word per hour. Famous physicist, Niels Bohr once lamented Dirac as a man who knew plenty of physics, but barely said anything. Being extremely shy, Dirac almost rejected the Nobel Prize because he did not want the publicity. He only relented when his colleagues advised him that rejecting the prize would attract more publicity. When he finally arrived to receive the Nobel Prize, he had a roomful of committee members waiting while he sat at the railway station's waiting room. Dirac was more communicative with his family and was known to be a loving husband and good father. The first love letter he wrote was to his wife, Margit, who was said to be the opposite of him. Dirac's unconventional behavior might have left people around him confounded, but it also seemed to have contributed to his success as a physicist because of his extraordinary ability to focus.

Later years

Dirac retired in 1969 from Cambridge. In 1971 he held a professorship at Florida State University, Tallahassee, to be near his daughter Mary until his death at eighty-two. He was buried at the Roselawn Cemetery and has a commemorative marker in Westminster Abbey. Dirac was considered a founding father of modern quantum physics, and to date, his books remain standard reference works;

1930 - The Principles of Quantum Mechanics (1930): Explores the ideas of quantum mechanics using modern formalism that was mostly developed by Dirac. This textbook is still used today.

1966 - Lectures on Quantum Mechanics: Writes about quantum mechanics in curved space-time.

1966 - Lectures on Quantum Field Theory: The basics of quantum field theory adopting the Hamiltonian formalism.

1974 - Spinors in Hilbert Space: A series of lectures in 1969 given at the University of Miami.

1975 - General Theory of Relativity: A summary of Einstein's general theory of relativity.

Discoveries

- The Atomic Model and Quantum Mechanics - theorizing a new atomic model.
- Quantum Electrodynamics (QED)
- The Dirac Equation and Antimatter - a theory that combined quantum mechanics to describe the subatomic world.

CHAPTER 5

RICHARD FEYNMAN

"The first principle is that you must not fool yourself and you are the easiest person to fool." -Richard Feynman

11 May 1918 - 15 February 1988

<u>Early life</u>

Richard Phillips Feynman was born in Queens, New York City. His father was Melville Arthur Feynman, a sales manager, and mother, Lucille née Phillips, a housewife. Both his parents were Jewish. Feynman had a younger sister Joan whom he was close to and, upon his encouragement, became an astrophysicist.

Feynman did not start speaking until he was three-years-old. As a young boy, he expressed interest in engineering and would spend time repairing radios; he even had an experimental laboratory. During grade school, Feynman created a self-made burglar alarm system at home.

Education

Feynman studied at Far Rockaway High School in Queens. In school, Feynman rapidly progressed to higher math, and later, a test determined his IQ at a respectable 125. Feynman declined to join the Mensa, stating that his IQ was average. At fifteen, Feynman learned various topics such as advanced algebra, trigonometry, analytic geometry, infinite series, and both differential and integral calculus on his own. He also experimented with math topics using his own notation, and special symbols.

Feynman's application to Columbia University was rejected because they had reached their maximum quota for Jewish students. As a result, he enrolled in the Massachusetts Institute of Technology, where he majored in electrical engineering before switching to physics. He published two papers in the Physical Review on cosmic rays and forces in molecules while at university. In 1939, Feynman graduated with a bachelor's degree and was named a Putnam fellow.

Feynman got a perfect score in physics for his entrance exams to Princeton University. When Feynman gave his first seminar at the university, his attendees included renowned scientists like Albert Einstein, John von Neumann, and Wolfgang Pauli. In 1942, Feynman received his Ph.D. from Princeton.

Marriage

One of the stipulations of Feynman's Princeton scholarship was that he had to be single, so he waited until he received his Ph.D. to marry his high school sweetheart, Arline Greenbaum, in June 1942. Feynman married Arline despite knowing that she was sick with incurable tuberculosis and not expected to live beyond two years. They married in the city office witnessed by a pair of strangers. After that, Feynman visited his wife every weekend at the Deborah Hospital.

Career

During World War II, Feynman was recruited to work on the Manhattan Project. He and his wife relocated to Albuquerque, New Mexico, to work on the atomic bomb. Later, Feynman was sent to Los Alamos, where he was in charge of the theoretical task and calculations of the proposed atomic bomb. During this time, Feynman's salary could not support their living expenses and his wife's medical bills, and they were forced to use Arline's savings. Every weekend he would borrow his friend's car to visit Arline in Albuquerque. On 16 June 1945, Feynman sat for hours with his wife until she finally passed away. After her death, Feynman immersed himself in his work.

After the Manhattan Project, Feynman worked as a professor at Cornell University in 1945. Around this time, he got the army psychiatrists to exempt him from the war on the grounds that he had a mental illness.

By 1949, Feynman, who was getting restless at Cornell moved on to become the professor of theoretical physics at the California Institute of Technology (Caltech) - where he remained for the rest of his career. He met Mary Louise Bell from Kansas, and they got married in June 1952. However, they often quarreled and had differing views resulting in divorce in 1958.

In September 1958, while in Geneva for an Atoms for a peace conference, Feynman met Gweneth Howarth from Yorkshire.

They married in September 1960 and had a son and an adopted daughter.

In 1965 along with, Shinichiro Tomonaga and Julian Schwinger, Feynman shared the Nobel Prize in physics for their work in quantum electrodynamics.

Later years

Many people did not know Feynman's reputation until he served as part of the team that investigated the failure of the 1986 space shuttle Challenger. Feynman passed away at sixty-nine after a long battle with cancer. His fame continued to grow after his death partly because of his two autobiographies of anecdotes titled;

- 1985 - Surely You're Joking, Mr. Feynman! (Adventures of a Curious Character) which became a bestseller
- 1988 - "What Do You Care What Other People Think?" Further Adventures of a Curious Character

Discoveries

- Feynman's path integral.
- Feynman diagrams - an approximation technique for physicists to do calculations.
- Quantum electrodynamics (Nobel Prize) - Feynman demonstrated that quantum electrodynamics is a constant relative theory of electromagnetic interactions and is consistent with the indicators observed in experiments.
- Feynman parton model of hadrons - a model for proton that helps one calculate predictions for sub-nuclear interactions of protons.

CHAPTER 6
ALBERT A. MICHELSON

"It appears, from all that precedes, reasonably certain that if there be any relative motion between the earth and the luminiferous ether, it must be small; quite small enough entirely to refute Fresnel's explanation of aberration." -Albert A. Michelson

19 December 1852 - 9 May 1931

<u>Early life</u>

Albert Abraham Michelson was born in Strzelno, Poland (formerly known as Prussia). His father was Samuel Michelson, a Jewish merchant, and his mother was Rozalia Przyłubska. At two, Michelson's family moved to the United States. Michelson grew up in Virginia City, Nevada, and San Francisco.

<u>Education and career</u>

Michelson studied high school in San Francisco, where he lived with his aunt, Henriette Levy. In 1869 Michelson was appointed to the United States Naval Academy under a special award from President Ulysses S. Grant. Throughout his four years at the academy, Michelson excelled in climatology, optics, and heat. Upon graduating, he spent two years at sea before becoming an instructor in chemistry and physics at the academy from 1875 to 1879. Michelson was appointed to the Nautical Almanac office in 1879. A year later, he took leave to further his studies in Europe. While in Europe, he began constructing an interferometer, which is a device used to split a beam of light into two. During this time, he also visited the universities in Berlin, Heidelberg, and France. After his return from Europe, he left the navy.

Back in the United States, Michelson became intrigued by sciences and, in particular, the challenge of measuring the speed of light. He started conducting his own experiments and demonstrations while at Annapolis. Michelson became a professor of physics at the Case School of Applied Science in Cleveland, Ohio, in 1883, where he focused on improvising the interferometer. It was here that he conducted the famous Michelson-Morley experiment with Edward Morley.

In 1889, Michelson became a professor at Clark University in Worcester, Massachusetts, and then in 1892, the first head of the department of physics at the University of Chicago, where he remained until his retirement in 1929.

In 1907, Michelson became the first American to receive a Nobel Prize in physics *"for his optical precision instruments and the spectroscopic and metrological investigations carried out with their aid"* (taken from nobelprize.org). His other awards included the Copley Medal from the Royal Society in 1907, the Henry Draper Medal in 1916, and the Gold Medal of the Royal

Astronomical Society in 1923 - a crater on the moon was even named after him.

Marriage

Michelson married Margaret Hemingway in 1877. Margaret's father was a wealthy stockbroker in New York. The couple had three children but divorced in 1898. A year later, he married, Edna Standon and they had three daughters. It was said that his second marriage was a happier one. Before his death, Michelson sent his lawyer to ask his ex-wife, Margaret, to forgive him for any suffering he might have caused her. It was said that Michelson had the reputation of being difficult, inconsiderate, overbearing, and aloof in his younger days, although he mellowed in his later years.

Later years

Michelson passed away at seventy-eight in Pasadena, California. After Michelson's passing, Albert Einstein praised him for forging new paths for the physicists, and the development of the theory of relativity.

Discoveries

- Michelson interferometer
- Developed the apparatus and standard for measuring the speed of light

CHAPTER 7

WERNER HEISENBERG

"Revere those things beyond science which really matter and about which it is so difficult to speak." -Werner Heisenberg

5 December 1901 - 1 February 1976

<u>Early life</u>

Werner Karl Heisenberg was born in Würzburg, Germany. His father was Kaspar Ernst August Heisenberg, a Professor of medieval and Modern Greek studies at the University of Munich. His mother was Annie Wecklein. Heisenberg was brought up in a Lutheran Christian family.

<u>Education</u>

In 1911, Heisenberg studied at the Maximilians-Gymnasium in Munich, where his teachers were impressed by his gifts in mathematics. Heisenberg entered the Ludwig Maximilian University of Munich and the Georg-August University of

Göttingen from 1920 to 1923, where he majored in mathematics and physics. At the University of Munich, he studied under, Arnold Sommerfeld, who was an expert on the quantum model of physics and atomic spectroscopy, and Wilhelm Wien. At the University of Göttingen, he studied under physicists Max Born, James Franck, and mathematics with David Hilbert. While still a student, he became assistant to physicist Max Born. After getting his doctorate, Heisenberg obtained the qualification to teach university level in Germany.

Career

Heisenberg was a Privatdozent at the University of Göttingen from 1924 to 1927 - as an independent who was qualified to examine and teach without holding a chair. Between 1924 and 1925, Heisenberg went on to research at the University of Copenhagen with, Niels Bohr, the director of the Institute of Theoretical Physics. There Heisenberg conducted his research and published his seminal paper. He was under the grant of the International Education Board Rocketfeller Foundation.

In 1926, Heisenberg was appointed lecturer in theoretical physics at the University of Copenhagen, and at twenty-six, he became the professor of theoretical physics at the University of Leipzig. In 1929, he gave lectures in the United States, India, and Japan. In 1941, he became a professor of physics and director of the Kaiser Wilhelm Institute for Physics at the University of Berlin.

In 1928, Albert Einstein nominated Heisenberg, Jordan, and Born for the Nobel Prize in physics. Heisenberg was awarded the Nobel Prize in 1932 for *"his creation of quantum mechanics that led to the discovery of allotropic forms of hydrogen."* During the 1930s, his work focused mainly on high energy cosmic rays, which led to his proposed theory of explosion showers.

1933 marked the National Socialist German Worker's Party, also known as the Nazi Party, rising to power. The Nazi Party's new policies excluded politically 'unreliable' and non-ethnic Germans such as Jews, Romanis, and Slavs (ethnic Serbs, Poles, and Russians, etc.,) from civil service. As a result, many academics and professors like Einstein, Born, and Schrödinger were dismissed. Heisenberg responded with peaceful interventions in the hope that the extreme manifestations were temporary. Eventually, Heisenberg himself became a target, and the Schutzstaffel (SS) journal called him a 'white Jew.' It was resolved through the help of Heisenberg's mother's family contact with the SS chief. The deal was that Heisenberg would be spared from personal attacks, but he would forego his promotion to succeed, Sommerfeld, at the University of Munich. Despite this, Heisenberg, who had strong national loyalty, did not want to leave Germany during the worst times of Hitler's regime and even turned down offers from universities in the United States and other countries.

During World War II, Heisenberg was drafted to work for the bureau of army weapons on nuclear energy, of which he took a leading role. Heisenberg's research team was unsuccessful in producing an atomic bomb or a reactor. Some rumors suggested that Heisenberg deliberately sabotaged and delayed the research efforts. Heisenberg's role in the war remained a controversy.

Toward the end of the war, Heisenberg and other physicists were captured by American intelligence and sent to England. Transcripts of their recorded conversation while in capture revealed that Heisenberg, along with others, were relieved that the Allies won the war. Apparently, Heisenberg did not want an atomic bomb but only an atomic pile to produce energy. He was released in 1946 and returned to Germany. Heisenberg resumed his directorship and, along with his colleagues, reorganized the Institute for Physics at Göttingen.

In 1951, Heisenberg became the scientific representative of the Federal Republic at the UNESCO conference to promote international scientific cooperation. In 1957, Heisenberg became part of the Göttinger Manifest team that opposed the Federal Republic of Germany building nuclear weapons. During this period, Heisenberg focused his work on searching for a comprehensive quantum field theory.

Marriage

Heisenberg married Elisabeth Schumacher in April 1937. They married four months after meeting at a musical recital, of which Heisenberg was an accomplished pianist and who enjoyed classical music. Elisabeth's father was a renowned economics professor in Berlin, and her brother, E. F. Schumacher, was a famous economist and author. The couple had seven children over thirteen years, including a pair of fraternal twins. In June 1939, he purchased a summer home at Urfeld am Walchensee in southern Germany for his family.

Later years

Heisenberg retired as director of the Max Planck Institute for Physics in 1970. In his late sixties, Heisenberg wrote his autobiography in a series of conversations during the course of his life; it was a huge success and published in several languages for the mass market. The English version of his book is called

'Physics and Beyond: Encounters and Conversations.' At seventy-four, Heisenberg passed away in his home from kidney cancer. He was buried in Munich Waldfriedhof cemetery, Germany.

Discoveries

- Formulated the quantum theory of ferromagnetism
- Neutron-proton model of the nucleus
- S-matrix theory in particle scattering
- Uncertainty or indeterminacy principle of 1927, which was one of the earliest breakthroughs to quantum mechanics

CHAPTER 8

ERNEST RUTHERFORD

"All of physics is either impossible or trivial. It is impossible until you understand it, and then it becomes trivial." -Ernest Rutherford

30 August 1871 - 19 October 1937

<u>Early life</u>

Ernest Rutherford was born in Spring Grove, New Zealand. His father was James Rutherford, a farmer. His mother, Martha Thompson, was from Essex, England, and was a school teacher. He was the fourth child from a big family of twelve children. As a young boy, his nickname was 'Ern.' After school, Rutherford would spend most of his time helping out at home with chores and milking the cows. During the weekends, he would go swimming at the creek with his brothers. Because money was scarce at home, Rutherford often found creative ways to make pocket money, such as bird-nesting.

Education

Rutherford's mother often emphasized the importance of education. At ten, he received his first science book at Foxhill School. That very first science bookmarked an important moment in his life. Rutherford became enthralled and had a thirst for the academics. As a young boy, he constructed a homemade mini canon which promptly exploded. In 1887, Rutherford won a scholarship to study at the private secondary school - Nelson Collegiate School. He participated in debates and played rugby until 1889.

In 1890, Rutherford, eighteen, received a scholarship to study at the Canterbury College in Christchurch. During this time, his professors spurred his eagerness to seek solid evidence through scientific experiments. Rutherford achieved first-class honors in math and science and received both his Bachelor of Arts and Master of Arts degree.

Marriage

During Rutherford's time at the Canterbury College, he fell in love with his landlady's daughter, Mary Newton. Upon getting his first job as a professor at Montreal, they married in 1900, and the couple had a daughter named Eileen.

Career

After Rutherford's graduation, he spent two years in research, where he invented a new type of radio receiver. In 1895, Rutherford was awarded the research fellowship from the Royal Commission for the Exhibition of 1851 and traveled for his postgraduate study at the Cavendish Laboratory at the University of Cambridge. At twenty-four, he studied under, J.J. Thompson a physicist and Nobel Laureate in physics. However, some of the conservative members became jealous of Rutherford because he was one of the rare researchers without a Cambridge degree. Nonetheless, encouraged by Thompson, Rutherford succeeded in detecting radio waves at half a mile and held the world record at that time.

In 1898, upon Thomson's recommendation, Rutherford got a position as a professor at the McGill University in Montreal, Canada. It was during his time at Montreal that led him to do the work that won him the Nobel Prize in chemistry in 1908. After nine years in Montreal, Rutherford took the chair of physics at the Victory University of Manchester, England, in 1907. During World War I (1914–18), Rutherford was working on a top-secret antisubmarine research. In 1919, when Thomson retired, Rutherford took over his position as the Cavendish professor of experimental physics at Cambridge, where he worked till the end of his life.

Other achievements

Rutherford was knighted in 1914 and appointed to the Order of merit in 1925. He was elected Fellow of the Royal Society in 1903 and became the president from 1925 - 1930. His countless honors included the Rumford Medal in 1905, the Copley Medal in 1922, and the Bressa Prize in 1910. He was also given honorary doctorates from universities like Cambridge, Oxford, Edinburg, Yale, Leeds, and Melbourne, and others.

During his lifetime, Rutherford published several books;

- Radioactivity
- Radioactive Transformations

- Radiation from Radioactive Substances
- The Electrical Structure of Matter
- The Artificial Transmutation of the Elements
- The Newer Alchemy

Later years

Rutherford, who was said to be the greatest physicist since Faraday was known to be a straightforward and no-nonsense person who spoke his mind. His boundless energy and enthusiasm often left his colleagues struggling to catch up with him. He died at the age of sixty-six at Cambridge from a strangulated hernia complication and was buried at Westminster Abbey.

Discoveries

Discovery of alpha and beta radiation. He coined the terms alpha, beta, and gamma for the three most common types of nuclear radiation, which is still used today.

Discovered radioactive elements have half-lives and coined the term half-life period. Rutherford received a Nobel Prize in chemistry for his investigations into radioactive substances.

- The age of planet Earth and radiometric dating - to find out how old things are
- Discovery of the atomic nucleus using the gold foil experiment
- Discovery of nuclear reactions - $14N + \alpha \rightarrow 17O + 1H$
- Discovery of the proton - $14N + \alpha \rightarrow 17O + proton$
- Predicting the existence of the neutron

CONCLUSION

Thank you for reading this book.

I hope this book has been an eye-opener giving you a glimpse into the lives and minds of the world's great scientists from across the ages who have given their blood and sweat to advance the world of science.

Yours truly,

LEE KHENG CHOOI

Printed in the United States
By Bookmasters